Good Citizens

HEINLE
CENGAGE Learning

Y|S|G
A YBM COMPANY
Young & Son
Global, Inc.

How do you help your friends?

Contents

Vocabulary

citizens

help

share

4

fairly

obey

clean

Citizens

We live in a community.

Good citizens make our community a better place.

How can you be a good citizen?

Helping

Good citizens help others.
Your friend has hurt her leg.
You can help your friend
carry her books.

Sharing

Good citizens share with others.
Your friend has no umbrella.
You can share your umbrella
with your friend.

Playing Fairly

Good citizens play fairly.

You want to win a soccer game.

You should not break rules to win.

Obeying Laws

Good citizens obey laws.
You want to cross the street.
You should wait for the green light.

Keeping the Community Clean

Good citizens keep the community clean.

The community park is dirty.

You can help to pick up trash.

Communities need good citizens.
You can be a good citizen, too!

What do good citizens do?

Like Good Citizens Do

We can all be good citizens.
Let's find out what to do.
They always obey laws.
They always play fairly.
Now you know what you can do
To be a good citizen, too!

We can all be good citizens.
Let's find out what to do.
They always help others.
They always like to share.
Now you know what you can do
To be a good citizen, too!

Index